D0274148

VOLUME 3

PSALMS

SONGS FROM THE HEART

10 Publishing
a division of 10 of those.com

Unless otherwise stated, Scripture quotations are taken from THE HOLY BIBLE, NEW INTERNATIONAL VERSION (Anglicised Edition). Copyright © 1979, 1984, 2011 by Biblica (formerly International Bible Society). Used by permission of Hodder & Stoughton Publishers. All rights reserved. 'NIV' is a registered trademark of Biblica. UK trademark number 1448790.

Copyright © 2018 by Graham Hooper

First published in Great Britain in 2018

The right of Graham Hooper to be identified as the Author of this Work has been asserted by him in accordance with the Copyright, Designs and Patents Act 1988.

All rights reserved. No part of this publication may be reproduced, stored in a retrieval system or transmitted in any form or by any means, electronic, mechanical, photocopying, recording or otherwise, without the prior permission of the publisher or a licence permitting restricted copying.

British Library Cataloguing in Publication Data

A record for this book is available from the British Library

ISBN: 978-1-912373-42-0
Designed by Diane Warnes
Printed in the UK

10Publishing, a division of 10ofthose.com
Unit C, Tomlinson Road, Leyland, PR25 2DY, England
Email: info@10ofthose.com
Website: www.10ofthose.com

Graham Hooper

54 UNDATED DEVOTIONS
THROUGH PSALMS 101–150

INTRODUCTION

Structure

The book of psalms is a collection of 150 psalms (songs and poems), divided up into five smaller 'books' as follows:

- Book 1: Psalms 1–41;
- Book 2: Psalms 42–72;
- Book 3: Psalms 73–89;
- Book 4: Psalms 90–106; and
- Book 5: Psalms 107–150.

There are some identifiable groupings of psalms around specific themes, and it is helpful to understand the overall context when we study one particular psalm within any one of these groupings. For example:

- the focus of Psalms 93–100 is on the Lord as the great King;
- Psalms 113–118 form the Hallel, traditionally sung on Passover night;
- Psalms 120–134 are the 'songs of ascents' for pilgrims; and
- Psalms 146–150 close out the book with songs of praise.

Recurring themes

Some powerful themes recur though the psalms: the sovereignty, justice and faithful love of God; why evil people seem to prosper; personal trust and commitment to the promises of God in the face of difficulty; and the greatness of the power of the Creator God – the rock, the refuge, the fortress and the one worthy of our trust, our praise and our worship.

There is also some repetition of words and phrases and even of some whole psalms. For example:

- Psalm 53 is the same as Psalm 14 apart from a few details and the greater part of verse 5 of Psalm 53;
- Psalm 70 is practically identical to Psalm 40:13–17; and
- Psalm 108 is made up of two psalm endings: 57:7–11 and 60:5–12.

Style

The psalms are poetry and songs. Many contain poetic imagery. They include praise, thanksgiving, questioning, requests and laments, but rarely instruction.

Some psalms are written in the form of acrostics. For example, in the very long Psalm 119 each section begins with a different letter of the Hebrew alphabet. In Psalm 34 each verse begins with a different letter.

Who wrote the psalms?

Many of the psalms tell us (in their header) who wrote them. 73 of the 150 psalms are attributed to David, the shepherd boy who became king. Several were written by Asaph, a temple musician, and some by the Sons of Korah, a guild of temple officials. Others are attributed to authors such as Solomon (Ps. 72) and Moses (Ps. 90), or are unattributed (for example, Ps. 1).

When were the psalms written?

The simple answer seems to be over a period between the time of David (1000 BC approximately) – though with the psalm attributed to Moses possibly earlier – and the years after the exile of the people of Judah into Babylon (300–500 BC). In some cases the headers tell us about the circumstances in which the psalms were written. For example, the note at the head of Psalm 51 tells us that David's famous prayer of repentance was a response to God after the prophet Nathan had confronted him with his sins of adultery and murder. Similarly, we are told that David wrote Psalm 3 while on the run from his own son Absalom who was trying to kill him.

The psalms in the New Testament

The psalms formed the 'hymnbook' of Israelite religion before the time of Christ. There are over 50 quotations from the psalms in the New Testament – more than any other Old Testament book. The frequent use of quotations from 'messianic psalms' in the book of Acts shows us how many of the psalms prophetically point to the coming Messiah and have a specific fulfilment in Jesus Christ. Jesus frequently quoted from the psalms as part of God's Word and as revealing truth about himself (see, for example, Luke 24:44).

The psalms in the Christian church

From the very beginning of the Christian church the psalms have been accepted as part of the divine revelation, and have been used widely in personal and corporate prayers and praise for the past two thousand years. As we read the psalms, therefore, with the New Testament in our hand, we can expect to learn more about Jesus.

The value and use of the psalms today

The psalms form part of our inspired Scripture. When we read them with an open, prayerful heart, we will find that the God who inspired them will continue to speak through them today. He speaks to us where we are at. He challenges us, encourage us, and stirs up our faith and commitment to him.

Like all good poetry, the psalms engage the heart and emotions as well as the mind. Their continuing widespread use in study, private prayer and communal worship is testament to their ongoing appeal to believers in every culture. Whatever our experience at any given time in the emotional spectrum, from elated joy to deep depression, we can find a psalm which echoes our experience. It's no wonder that at times when we find it hard to read or study other parts of the Bible – when we are tired, sick or depressed – it is to the psalms that we turn. They help us to pray, to worship and to reflect on God and our relationship with him.

As we read them, study them, pray them or sing them, our God delights to use them to reveal to us more about himself and to deepen our knowledge of him.

Studying the psalms with this guide

Read the psalm for the day and then the notes and questions contained in the study guide. Ask yourself some questions as you read:

- What do I learn about God in this verse and passage?
- What did this mean to the original hearers?
- What does it mean for me in the twenty-first century?
- How can I respond with practical action?

A leader worth following

Think of a leader that you really respect, maybe in politics, business, sport or at church. What particular qualities do they have that you admire? What makes them worth following?

The leader's commitment

It's common for anyone taking on a leadership role to make clear what they stand for, and the direction they want to take, in some sort of public commitment. Politicians are sworn in, officials in organisations sign codes of ethics, coaches of sports team set their goals and team values. Parents, at the baptism or dedication of their children, make public promises about how they will bring up their children

Even if we are not required to make any public statements, even if we are taking on a very minor leadership role, it's good to get clear in our mind what we stand for and what we will commit to do. This psalm, one of only two psalms of David in Book 4 (103 is the other), is about leadership.

There are seven statements beginning 'I will' in the first four verses, which can be summarised as:

- commitment to worship God (v. 1);

- commitment to integrity at work and at home (vv. 2–3); and

- resolve to steer clear of obvious sin and evil (v. 4).

The leader's actions

We've seen David's personal values and commitments. What matters more to the people he leads, though, is how he will exercise his power. What will he actually do and how will it affect them? David states that he:

- won't tolerate people who slander others or think too highly of themselves (v. 5);

- will surround himself with loyal, faithful people (v. 6); and

- won't associate with deceitful, lying, double-dealing people (v. 7).

REFLECTION

It's one thing to start out in a leadership role with high ideals. It's another to see it through under pressure. Sadly David failed to live up to his commitments, as we may fail to live up to ours. His great successor, Jesus, lived out what he promised, and gave his life out of love and faithfulness for us. He is uniquely a leader worth following.

Two different perspectives

We may view exactly the same set of circumstances in very different ways depending on our personality, our mood and our ability to cope at the time. In an optimistic mood, we might see the glass half full. In our more pessimistic moments, the same glass looks half empty.

This psalm gives us two very different perspectives, not so much glass half empty or half full, but more like completely empty (vv. 1–11) or completely full (vv. 12–27). What makes the difference? Getting a clear view of God's almighty power and presence.

The first half of the psalm is a picture of deep, prolonged suffering. It begins like many other psalms (for example, Ps. 61:1 and 64:1) with a plea to God to listen to David's cry for help (v. 1). His body is in pain and wasting away (vv. 3–6). He can't sleep or hear (v. 7). On top of all that, he is being taunted by cruel enemies who have trashed his good reputation (v. 8). Worse still, he feels that God is angry with him and has cast him aside (v. 10). The focus is very definitely on 'I', 'me', 'my' – the psalmist is very wrapped up in himself and his problems.

'But ...' As in so many psalms, halfway through there is a radical change. The focus shifts from the individual to the unseen, eternal, almighty God, and from the individual to God's people (v. 12). The psalmist is now confident that God will arise and have compassion on the city ('Zion', v. 13) and the people, and that the nations and kings of the earth will revere God (v. 15). The Lord will rebuild the city; he will respond to the prayers of the desolate (vv. 16–17). The great God is the Creator of all (vv. 25–27).

The use of these three verses in Hebrews 1:10–12 shows that this is a messianic psalm, pointing to Jesus. He suffered (vv. 1–11; see also Ps. 22) and was raised up to glory.

REFLECTION

There are two clear messages here for all of us. First, however deep our trouble, God stays faithful. Second, we are reminded of our Lord Jesus Christ, who endured great suffering ... for us.

 **DAY 3**

Praising and blessing God

When our minds are distracted and our spirits are dull, the psalms prompt us to praise God, deliberately turning our focus away from ourselves and towards him.

What God has done

Psalm 103 helps us call to mind all that God has done. He has:

- forgiven our sins and healed our diseases (v. 3);

- redeemed our lives 'from the pit' and crowned us 'with love and compassion' (v. 4);

- provided for us (v. 5);

- continued to work by his Holy Spirit to lift and renew our spirits when we are worn out (v. 5); and

- spoken and acted in history so that we can know him (v. 7).

Then, as if remembering again the sinfulness, selfishness and stubbornness of humankind, the psalmist celebrates the wonderful compassion of God, who 'does not treat us as our sins deserve' (v. 10) and whose love is greater than we can ever imagine (v. 11). Does God keep a record of our wrongdoings and failings? No! He completely takes them away (v. 12). Is that enough to get us praising God? Psalm 103 has much more!

What God is like

We are encouraged to praise God for what he is like. He cares for the oppressed and disadvantaged of this world (v. 6). He is a loving Father who cares about his children, and who knows how we are wired and all our weaknesses (vv. 13–14). This life may be as short and uncertain as the flowers of the field, here today and gone tomorrow (vv. 15–16), but God is eternal and his love goes on for ever (v. 17). Is God really in charge of this world? Yes: 'his kingdom rules over all' (v. 19). That is why the psalmist calls everyone and everything that God has made to join in praise of their maker and Lord (vv. 20–21).

REFLECTION

Read Psalm 103. Then list all the reasons you have to praise God and turn that into worship.

Praise to the great Creator

When we take time on holiday to enjoy God's creation, whether walking, sailing, cycling or just relaxing on the beach, our mood can quickly change when our holiday ends. Getting back to the routine of work, relationship problems at home and the barrage of bad news on TV may bring us crashing back to earth.

This lovely psalm reflects that experience. The first 34 verses celebrate the beauty, grandeur and purity of God's amazing creation. But in verse 35 the psalmist remembers that sin and evil have not gone away. He longs that they would 'vanish from the earth'.

The psalm retells the creation story of Genesis 1 in roughly the same order. God created:

- the light (v. 2);

- the earth (v. 5);

- the waters (vv. 6–10), vegetation and trees (vv. 14–17);

- the sun, moon and stars (vv. 19–23);

- creatures of sea and air (vv. 25–26); and

- animals and humans (vv. 21–24); as well as

- food and drink to enjoy (vv. 14–15, 27–28).

In describing God's creation in verses 1–9 the psalmist uses his own God-given creative gift of poetry. He describes the heavens as stretched out 'like a tent' (v. 2) and the clouds like a chariot riding 'on the wings of the wind' (v. 3). He pictures the streams running away from the thunder, flowing down to the valleys from the high mountains (vv. 7–8).

Verses 10–19 describe more prosaically how God provides his creatures with food and drink (vv. 11–14) to satisfy their basic needs, and to help enjoy life (v. 15)! Humans work (v. 23) and trade (v. 26), but it is the hand of the Creator that supplies our need (vv. 27–28). It is the Lord who breathes life into every human being (vv. 29–30). As the psalmist ponders the infinite variety and grandeur of this world, he reflects on the greatness of the Creator (v. 24) and prays that the thoughts expressed in his poem would be pleasing to him (v. 34).

REFLECTION

As we worship God for creating such a wonderful world, we also look forward to the fulfilment of his promise to create a new heaven and a new earth, completely free from sin and evil (Matt. 13:41; Rev. 21). The psalmist's prayer (v. 35) will be answered when Christ returns.

Praise to the Redeemer

In the busyness of life it's good to stop sometimes to take stock, looking back to what God has done for us and how he has led us to this point.

With our Bible in our hand we look back at what God has said and done *in history*, supremely in sending us his Son, Jesus the Saviour. With our photo album or diary in our hand, or with just our memories, it's also good to remind ourselves what God has done *in our own lives*. This backward look serves to strengthen our faith to keep going and to keep trusting. So it is with this psalm. Psalms 105 and 106 form a pair. Both look back over Israel's history. But whereas Psalm 106 dwells on the failures of God's people, this psalm focuses on the great faithfulness of God. Note the psalmist had no concept of private religion, but rather the opposite: the joy of knowing God is to be celebrated and shared.

He begins with a series of exhortations (vv. 1–6):

- give praise and make God known (v. 1);

- sing and tell of 'his wonderful acts' (v. 2);

- glory and rejoice in the Lord (v. 3);

- look to the Lord and 'seek his face' (v. 4); and

- remember all he has done (v. 5).

Then he looks back over the history of Israel, not in terms of human accomplishment, but as a series of God's mighty acts (vv. 7–45). He recalls God's covenant with Abraham, Isaac and Jacob to be their God and to give them a land (vv. 8–15). He remembers Joseph (vv. 17–22) and the growth of the children of Jacob, renamed Israel, in Egypt (vv. 23–25); the deliverance from Egypt led by Moses (vv. 26–38); and God's guidance and provision on their journey through the wilderness (vv. 39–41). Finally, he celebrates again that God kept his promise to Abraham (v. 42).

REFLECTION

Echo the words of John Newton's famous hymn, 'Amazing Grace':

Through many dangers, toils and snares,

I have already come,

'Tis grace that brought me safe thus far

and grace will lead me home.

 **DAY 6**

Our longsuffering God

'Won't you ever learn?!' You may have heard that in your childhood or adolescence from an exasperated parent or teacher when you made the same mistake for the second, third or fourth time. It's a comment that God might well address to us when we repeatedly fail to learn the lessons he tries to teach us.

This psalm is about God's patience over long periods with his people who found it difficult to obey even the simplest instruction. But, thankfully, it's not all bad news. The psalm begins and ends with thankfulness for God's love, which 'endures for ever' (v. 1).

As the psalmist looks back to God's people who failed in the past, he admits that he is no better: 'We have sinned, even as our ancestors did' (v. 6). Like the writer of Psalm 78, he looks back over Israel's history of failure to keep their covenant with God, bringing to mind all their sins and failures. In each instance, however, he also recognises God's patient faithfulness:

- in delivering Israel from Egypt (vv. 6–12). The Israelites 'did not remember your many kindnesses' and rebelled (v. 7), yet God saved them, leading them out of Egypt and across the Red Sea, and rescuing them from the pursuing Egyptian army (vv. 9–11). For a short time they 'sang his praise' (v. 12), but it didn't last.

- in the wilderness (vv. 13–33). The people grumbled and 'soon forgot what he had done' (v. 13). They turned to idolatry and made a golden calf to worship (vv. 19–23). They envied Moses and Aaron, who had been entrusted by God with leadership (v. 16). They completely 'forgot the God who saved them' (v. 21).

- in the Promised Land (vv. 34–39). The Israelites compromised their worship of God, adapted to the culture of the neighbouring tribes and worshipped their idols (vv. 34–39). Yet even then God delivered them, remembering his covenant (v. 45) and even causing their captors 'to show them mercy' (v. 46).

REFLECTION

This last psalm in Book 4 of the psalms ends with praise to God who is patient with failing, sinful, grumbling, faithless people... like us (see 2 Pet. 3:9).

Unfailing love

What happens when God answers our desperate cries for help and brings us relief? Do we forget it and move on? Do we tell people it was just good luck, coincidence or 'the way things turned out'? Psalm 107 is a reminder to stop and thank God when he answers prayer.

This psalm opens the fifth and final book of psalms (Ps. 107–150), which are generally on a note of praise. The opening verse sets the tone: 'Give thanks to the LORD for he is good; his love endures for ever.' The psalm then encourages all believers to speak out their faith in praise and testimony: 'Let the redeemed of the LORD tell their story' (v. 2).

The writer looks back on history and looks around his world to people crying out to God for help in desperate situations. There are refugees with no home (vv. 4–9); prisoners (vv. 10–16); foolish people who refused the Lord's authority (vv. 17–19); and business travellers, sailors and merchants, whose travels involved high risk, even life-threatening, situations (vv. 23–32). In each case the psalm remembers, like a chorus repeated through a song, two aspects. First, 'Then they cried out to the LORD in their trouble, and he delivered them from their distress' (vv. 6, 13, 19, 28). Second, 'Let them give thanks to the LORD for his unfailing love and his wonderful deeds for mankind' (vv. 8, 15, 21, 31).

In the last section (vv. 32–42) the psalmist looks back with great thankfulness at God's goodness in providing food and prosperity, and in coming to the aid of those humbled by struggle and sorrow.

REFLECTION

Psalm 107 ends with this statement: 'Let the one who is wise heed these things and ponder the loving deeds of the LORD' (v. 43). Take a few moments to look back over the times God has answered your prayers, and thank him for his unfailing love in the Lord Jesus Christ: his saving death and resurrection, and the promise of his return.

Facing a new challenge

At first sight this psalm seems to be a simple cut-and-paste job, joining together the second half of Psalm 57 with the second half of Psalm 60. But a closer look shows that David has reworked this material with the specific intent of encouraging God's people when facing either personal opposition (which was the subject of Ps. 57:1–6) or a threat to the people as a whole (Ps. 60). He reminds them that their hope lies in dependence on God and on his steadfast love. It's therefore a psalm for a new situation; an inspiration and encouragement for a new challenge.

The psalm begins with a statement of faith by the king, the anointed leader: 'My heart, O God, is steadfast' (v. 1), and ends with the people together confidently asserting, 'With God we shall gain the victory' (v. 13). The reason for his hope in the face of serious difficulty is not glass-half-full optimism, but rather his reliance on the steadfast love of God (vv. 4, 6).

He calls on the temple band, and all the surrounding nations, to join in praise (vv. 2–3). He is taken up with the prospect of God's greatness and love (vv. 4–5), which is 'higher than the heavens'. He calls for God's help (v. 6), but remembers that all God's people, the land, the surrounding tribes and even the traditional enemies of God's people (Moab, Edom and Philistia) are under the control of God (vv. 7–9).

Then he comes back down to earth in verses 10–13. After this heavenly view of the power of God and the glory of God covering all the earth (v. 5), he is confronted by the immediate challenge that God's people face serious opposition. They feel that God is no longer with them and helping them to fight their battles (v. 11). He calls again for God's help, recognising that 'human help is worthless' (v. 12) and their only hope is total reliance on God (v. 13).

REFLECTION

In the words of Paul in the New Testament, 'when I am weak, then I am strong' (2 Cor. 12:10). He knew that God's power is made perfect in human weakness (2 Cor. 12:8).

A cry for vengeance

If you have ever been hurt – really hurt – emotionally or physically, you have most probably experienced the strong human desire for payback, which is the theme of this psalm. In their purest form such desires are a cry for justice: for the guilty to be punished and wrongs to be righted. In their worst form they show vindictive hatred and cruel intent, a desire for revenge that has prolonged many personal and family feuds, and even started many wars.

Perhaps this psalm, and others like it (such as Psalms 35 and 137), leaves us feeling quite battered. Yet it is written not as a pattern for us to follow, but for our learning. We *can* pour out our deepest feelings to God. Remember too that it was written by the king, a person with public responsibility for justice.

In verses 1–5 David shares with God, and with us, his deep pain. He has been slandered by 'people who are wicked and deceitful' (v. 1). They have attacked him with 'words of hatred' and 'without cause' (v. 3). He had befriended these people, but they now 'repay me evil for good, and hatred for my friendship' (v. 5).

So, in verses 6–20, David asks God to repay them according to what they have done to him. Notice that there is no indication that David is going to take revenge himself. He asks God to act and leaves that to him.

The whole mood changes in verses 21–26 as David now asks God to help him. He is in a desperate state, physically, emotionally and spiritually. He calls on God's 'unfailing love' (v. 26), his covenant commitment to save and keep his people. He asks that God's blessing on him will put his enemies to shame (vv. 28–29).

Finally, in verses 30–31, David makes clear his commitment to worship, honour and praise the Lord whatever happens because God 'stands at the right hand of the needy, to save their lives from those who would condemn them'.

REFLECTION

Whether or not we use these prayers to tell God our true feelings, we need to heed the command of Jesus: 'love your enemies and pray for those who persecute you' (Matt. 5:44), a command he himself obeyed (Luke 23:34).

The King and the Priest

This song of David is full of surprises. First, King David is addressing another royal person as 'my lord' (v. 1). What sort of person other than God would David address like that?

Second, this king is also a priest, a double role not allowed in the Law of Moses. Only men from the tribe of Levi were allowed to be priests (Num. 8:5–11). But this king is in the line of Melchizedek (v. 4), an enigmatic figure who appears in Genesis as a priest to whom Abraham presented gifts (Gen. 14:18–20; Heb. 5:5–10; 7:11–17).

The King

Jesus tells us that this psalm spoke prophetically about him. In Mark 12:36 Jesus quotes this psalm, in which David was 'speaking by the Holy Spirit' about the coming King (Messiah), to point out to the Jewish leaders that Scripture foresaw the Messiah as both a *descendant* of David and *one greater* than David. Peter, speaking on the day of Pentecost, also quotes this psalm in demonstrating that Jesus was the promised Messiah (Acts 2:33–35).

The Priest

A priest represents the people to God and acts as an intermediary between God and the people. Jesus, the King of Kings, is also the great High Priest who alone can give us access into the very presence of God. He is unique. He did not have to sacrifice for his own sin (he was without sin) and his offering of his own life as a sacrifice for sin was once, for all and for ever. When the Old Testament priests went into the sanctuary to make their offerings, they remained standing (Heb. 10:11). By contrast when Jesus took his rightful place at the right hand of the Father, he sat down (Heb. 10:12), signifying that he had completed the work his Father had given him to do (Heb. 7:23–28).

REFLECTION

Read this psalm together with the passages in Hebrews. Think of what it means that Jesus is both our King (the ultimate authority) and Priest (who opens up access to God for us).

 **DAY 11**

Character, words and deeds

Both Psalms 111 and 112 are acrostics, each having 22 lines (10 verses in our English Bibles) and each one beginning with successive letters of the Hebrew alphabet. While Psalm 111 focuses on the character and works of God, Psalm 112 paints a portrait of a godly believer. They are two sides of the same coin.

This psalm begins with a public commitment of faith (v. 1). It ends with the familiar phrase from the book of Proverbs (see 1:7 and 9:10): 'The fear of the LORD is the beginning of wisdom' (v. 10). In the middle (vv. 2–9) there are eight couplets of sayings, all extolling the virtues of the Lord in terms of what he is like (his character), what he has done (his deeds) and what he has said (his words).

As fallible human beings, what we say is not always consistent with what we do, and what we say and do often reveal a side of our character that we would rather others didn't see. But with God there is a wonderful consistency and harmony between his character, his actions and his words, and this is celebrated in this psalm.

We see this consistency in his:

• character: 'his righteousness endures for ever' (v. 3)';

• commitment to his people: 'he remembers his covenant for ever' (v. 5; see also v. 9); and

• words: 'all his precepts are trustworthy' (v. 7; see also v. 8).

So, fittingly, praise of him will continue for ever (v. 10). Further, just as all that God does shows his righteous, faithful and just character (vv. 3, 7), so his laws are 'enacted in faithfulness and uprightness' (v. 8).

REFLECTION

This psalm encourages us to ponder what God has done (v. 2) in history (v. 3), in providing for us (v. 5) and redeeming us (v. 9). It should cause us to delight in what he has said in his Word (vv. 7–8), and in the total consistency and perfection of his character. We find all of this in God's self-revelation in the Bible. Perhaps best of all, we are encouraged to remember and celebrate his grace and compassion (v. 4) in making fallible sinners like us his own people (vv. 5, 9).

 **DAY 12**

The godly believer

We saw in Psalm 111 a beautiful description of the consistency and perfection of God, in his character, words and deeds. This psalm focuses on the believer.

In his 'Sermon on the Mount' (Matt. 5–7) Jesus called his followers to 'Be perfect ... as your heavenly Father is perfect' (Matt. 5:48) and to love even their enemies (Matt. 5:44) – a great test of character! How is that to happen? When we think about the selfishness and inconsistency of our character, we might well ask! Wonderfully, the New Testament encourages us with the good news that God's purpose for our lives is to change us to become more like him (1 Thess. 5:23). Jesus died that we might be forgiven and experience the power of his risen life. His Spirit is given to begin the work of changing us into his likeness (2 Cor. 3:18), a process begun in this life and which will be complete in the next.

If ever we are tempted to believe the devil's lie that this new way of life somehow spoils or constricts us, then this psalm is a great remedy. The godly life is one of blessing (vv. 1–3), of generosity (vv. 5, 9), of trust rather than fear (vv. 7–8) and of light even in the dark times (v. 4).

It opens (like Psalm 1 and the book of Job) with an idyllic picture of prosperity and enjoyment in daily life (vv. 2–3) for those who:

• 'fear the LORD' and 'find great delight in his commands' (v. 1);

• are gracious and compassionate to others, reflecting God's grace and compassion to them (v. 4);

• are generous (v. 5) and have 'freely scattered their gifts to the poor' (v. 9); and

• 'conduct their affairs with justice' (v. 5).

Such people are blessed in their family life and home. They are not immune from bad experiences, but they will not fear bad news and will not be shaken because 'their hearts are steadfast, trusting in the LORD' (v. 7).

REFLECTION

Notice the contrast in this psalm (similar to Psalm 1) between the righteous and the wicked. God's blessing is on the righteous but 'the longings of the wicked will come to nothing' (v. 10).

Worthy of praise

It may seem a strange thing to a non-believer that Christians should voice words of thanks and praise to a being we cannot see. Are we just floating words out into an empty universe? The reason we praise is because we believe the invisible God has revealed himself to us in his creation (Ps. 19), in his spoken Word, in his mighty acts in history and supremely in sending us his Son (Heb. 1:1–3). Praise starts as a response to what God has revealed about himself in the Bible. There is a God. He is good and worthy of our praise.

Psalm 113 is the first in a series of six psalms comprising the Hallel, which were traditionally sung on Passover night. All six celebrate the deliverance of Israel from slavery in Egypt. According to custom, Psalms 113–114 were sung before the Passover meal and Psalms 115–118 afterwards. It may well be that this was the 'hymn' sung by Jesus on the night before his death, after he had celebrated Passover together with his friends (Mark 14:26).

Psalms 111–113 all begin with 'Hallelujah!', or 'Praise the LORD' as we have in most English translations. Psalm 113 begins and ends on a note of praise and gives us reasons why God is so praiseworthy. He is unimaginably great, 'exalted over all the nations, his glory above the heavens' (vv. 4–5), and yet he 'raises the poor from the dust and lifts the needy from the ash heap' (v. 7). Verses 7–8 are almost exact quotes from Hannah's song of praise (1 Sam. 2:8) when God answered her prayers for a child. No wonder the psalmist asks rhetorically in amazement: 'Who is like the LORD our God?' (v. 5).

REFLECTION

The God revealed in the Bible is strikingly different from the 'gods' of other religions, past and present. He is both great and gracious, and invites us to respond in worship, faith and obedience on both counts.

 **DAY 14**

The presence of the Lord

We have seen how Psalm 113 celebrates the grace and greatness of God. Psalm 114 looks back to Israel's deliverance from slavery in Egypt to show us how God's greatness and grace work out in human experience. But the focus is not so much on the Exodus event, with its great deliverance and miracles, as on God's presence with his people (vv. 2, 7). He did not deliver them and then leave them alone to get on as best they could. He delivered them to make them his people and to live among them (v. 2). It is very significant that the book of Exodus, which begins with the Israelites suffering in Egypt and tells of their deliverance from Egypt and the giving of the Law at Mount Sinai, ends with the glory of God in the midst of the people (Ex. 40:34–38).

Verses 3–8 paint an extravagant poetic picture of the sea retreating, the rivers turned back, and the mountains and hills skipping like spring lambs. What causes this response from God's creation (vv. 5–6)? It is the 'presence of the God of Jacob' (v. 7). The creation is welcoming the Creator as he comes to live on earth. We find a similar picture in the New Testament, where Paul describes the creation longing for God to come and set this broken, corrupted world to rights; it is waiting 'on tiptoe'[1] to welcome back the Creator to wind up human history (Rom. 8:20–22).

This psalm celebrates the presence of the Lord God – the Creator and Redeemer – among his people. He is 'the God of Jacob', the name of God which is for ever a reminder that God made promises to his people and keeps them.

REFLECTION

We learn about God by meditating on his words and works in the Bible, and by singing his praises. We know God's presence now in the Holy Spirit (Rom. 5:5). In heaven we will enjoy God's presence for ever (Rev. 21:3–4).

One true God – our help and shield

This psalm expresses a deep sense of wonder and praise at the greatness of the covenant-keeping God. We cannot see him, but his love and faithfulness are to be experienced by all who trust him: 'Not to us, LORD, not to us but to your name be the glory, because of your love and faithfulness' (v. 1).

Verses 2–8 remind us that we worship an invisible God. Building idols to worship, or even as an aid to worship, is expressly forbidden in the Ten Commandments (Ex. 20:4–5). So, naturally enough, other cultures and nations might ask, 'Where is [your] God?' (v. 2). We cannot see him. Is he real?

But this psalm sees clearly that gods made by human hands cannot be gods at all (vv. 4–7). With penetrating insight the psalmist observes, 'Those who make them will be like them, and so will all who trust in them' (v. 8). By contrast, 'Our God is in heaven' (v. 3). So there is a three-fold call to the Israelites, to the House of Aaron and to all who fear him to 'trust in the LORD' because 'he is their help and shield' (vv. 9–11).

There follows a statement that 'The LORD remembers us and will bless us ... he will bless those who fear the LORD – small and great alike' (vv. 12–13). Verses 14–15 are a prayer of blessing, such as we may pray for others: 'May the LORD cause you to flourish ... May you be blessed by the LORD'. Then verse 16 reminds us, 'The highest heavens belong to the LORD, but the earth he has given to the human race.'

REFLECTION

As you pray, encourage yourself with the truth which is repeated three times in this psalm: 'trust in the LORD – he is [our] help and shield.' Praise God that all believers in Christ have God as their help and shield. As you pray for others, ask God to bring them to trust in the Lord and to know that he is their help and shield.

Thankfulness and commitment

A thankful heart is evidence that God is at work in our lives. Thankfulness is not specifically listed in the New Testament as a gift of the Holy Spirit, or even as a fruit of the Holy Spirit, but it is most surely a mark of God's work in someone's life. By contrast, grumbling, complaining and criticising others often comes very naturally to us. It shows how wrapped up in ourselves we can be. When we get like that, it's shows that we have forgotten God; we've forgotten how much he has given us and how much he has forgiven us. Reading the psalms, and turning them into our own prayers, is a great way to make thankfulness to God part of our worship and part of life.

Help in time of trouble (vv. 1–4)

The psalmist is thankful to God for answering his prayer in a time of great distress: 'I love the LORD, for he heard my voice; he heard my cry for mercy' (v. 1). He goes on to share his joy with all who will listen, and commits himself to keeping the promises he had made to God when in trouble.

A burst of praise (vv. 5–11)

The psalmist is also thankful that God is gracious and righteous and full of compassion (v. 5). He reminds himself again that the Lord has been good to him (vv. 7–8) and so he can be at rest in his soul.

Thankfulness and commitment (vv. 12–19)

As he remembers God's goodness, he asks himself what he can give God in return (v. 12). His answer is: 'I will lift up the cup of salvation and call on the name of the LORD. I will fulfil my vows to the LORD' (vv. 13–14), a promise repeated in verses 17–18. He knows that none of us have anything to offer God until we have first gratefully received his free offer of grace and mercy.

REFLECTION

When times are good, let's thank God. When life is difficult and thanking God does not come so easily, we can still be thankful that God is good and his love will never end.

 **DAY 17**

God's enduring love

These two psalms form the end of the Hallel (Psalms 113–118), traditionally sung at the Passover. Psalm 118 reads like a great processional. The crowd of pilgrims, most probably led by the king, would have sung these psalms as they approached the temple (v. 27). Psalm 117 celebrates God's unfailing, steadfast love. Psalm 118 begins and ends with thankfulness that God's love 'endures for ever'.

How had God's people experienced God's love in their lives? The psalmist looks back to God's rescue in the past (Ps. 118: 5, 13) as well as to his sustaining protection in the present (vv. 6–9) while surrounded by enemies (vv. 10–12). This may reflect the experience of an individual (probably the king) or of the nation, which experienced so much hatred and opposition. Note verses 15–16 refer back to the victory song of Moses, celebrating the power of the 'right hand' of God in the miraculous crossing of the Red Sea (see Ex. 15:6, 12). But these reflections can be echoed by God's people in every age. Three times the writer recalls how God had acted powerfully to rescue him: he was 'hard pressed' (v. 5), 'about to fall' (v. 13) and 'chastened ... severely' (v. 18), but God brought him through. You may be able to relate to that.

The frequent use of this psalm in the New Testament tells us that this is a messianic psalm, looking forward to the coming of Jesus. The crowds welcomed Jesus with the words of verse 26 as he rode into Jerusalem (Matt. 21:9). Later he was surrounded by enemies who hated him. He suffered, but won the victory – even over death. He was the 'stone the builders rejected' (v. 22; see also Matt. 21:42; Rom. 9:32), but God made him 'the cornerstone' (v. 22; see also Eph. 2:20; 1 Pet. 2:6). As Peter told the crowds on the the the day of Pentecost very directly, 'God has made this Jesus, whom you crucifed, both Lord and Messiah' (Acts 2:36).

REFLECTION

'... his love endures for ever.' This was not just a creed the psalmist had learned from his parents or religious teachers. It was his strongly held conviction. He had experienced God working in his life and saving God's people in many testing situations (vv. 5, 7, 10, 13).

An A–Z of godly living

This is a very long psalm! It comprises 22 eight-verse stanzas, with each stanza beginning with a successive letter of the Hebrew alphabet and each verse beginning with the 'headline' letter for that particular stanza.

How are we to understand it? How is it meant to be used? It's too long to sing, too long to pray in public worship and seems to have no clear logical flow to the thoughts expressed. It reads more like a succession of personal notes to self, like entries in a daily journal, and an intensely personal expression of the believer's relationship of faith with God. It's main focus is quite obviously on the Word of God, but its 176 verses contain several recurring themes:

- consciousness of sin (v. 176);

- love for the Word (v. 16; see also Ps. 19);

- faithfulness in the face of suffering and persecution (vv. 107, 153–157, 161);

- battling with setbacks and hard times (vv. 25, 28);

- being mocked and bullied by arrogant people (vv. 51, 69, 78, 85, 95); and

- longing for God (v. 41).

The psalm begins, very much like Psalm 1, with a description of a life blessed by God (vv. 1–3). The psalmist is aware that God's laws are 'to be fully obeyed' (v. 4), but as he looks at his own heart, he sees a failure to keep God's commands, a failure to live out the principles of the first four verses and a fear that God will therefore forsake him (v. 8). This is not legalism; it is the language of the covenant. Underlying the whole psalm is a deep joy to be found in a faith relationship with God who has spoken in his Word, the Bible (see Matt. 4:4).

REFLECTION

The psalmist prays, as we might, with deep longing for a steadfast heart (v. 5) and commits himself to praising God, learning from his Word and putting it into practice in his life (vv. 7–8).

God's Word in our hearts

I recently fulfilled a lifelong ambition to go trekking in Nepal. We visited a Buddhist training school for monks and watched boys as young as seven sitting at classroom desks, learning huge chunks of their sacred scriptures by heart. It made me feel quite lazy by comparison!

Have you ever learned passages of Scripture by heart? I recently met a Sri Lankan teacher who had memorised the whole of Psalm 119 in English. It's a great way to lock God's Word into our minds so we can press a recall button instantly and remind ourselves of God's truth wherever we are and whenever we choose.

It's one thing to memorise passages of Scripture, but this psalm takes us deeper: 'I have hidden your word *in my heart*' (v. 11, my italics). With the help of the Spirit of God, the psalmist meditates on it, turning it over in his mind: 'I meditate on your precepts and consider your ways' (v. 15). He speaks the Words of Scripture aloud, both to himself and to others (v. 13; see also Rom. 10:9). But this isn't a chore, a 'religious discipline'. It brings him great delight (vv. 14, 16). He is 'consumed with longing' (v. 20) for God's Word and he prays to God to teach him (v. 12) and to open his eyes to understand what he reads (v. 18).

As he sets himself to read, learn and obey God's words, he finds himself in a minority and becomes an object of scorn and contempt for unbelievers (vv. 21–23). He starts to feel like 'a stranger on earth' (v. 19). He knows he has to take a stand and he does: even though the rulers slander him, he will still hold fast to the Word of God and find delight in it (vv. 23–24).

REFLECTION

Read 1 Peter 2:11–12, written to Christians who, like the psalmist, were feeling like strangers in their society ('foreigners and exiles', v. 11), and were facing great opposition because of their faith and mockery because they no longer wanted to live as they had before (1 Pet. 4:4).

'Low in the dust'

What do you do when you are feeling really low? Phone a friend, sit at home alone with a glass of wine, chill out with your favourite music or just sit staring at the TV? If you are feeling energetic, you might go out to the gym or go out with friends to take your mind off your problems.

This psalmist turns to writing poetry! Thank God he did or we would not have had this wonderful psalm. He is 'laid low in the dust' (v. 25) and 'weary with sorrow' (v. 28). In this state he wisely turns to God and asks God to strengthen him (v. 28), to help him understand God's Word and to teach him (vv. 26, 29).

Unlike David in many of his psalms, this writer does not reveal what caused him to feel so low, though some of his prayers in this section give us a hint. He seems to have been tempted, and maybe had given in to temptation to follow 'deceitful ways' (v. 29), to chase after 'selfish gain (v. 36) and to waste his life chasing after 'worthless things' (v. 37). He was afraid of some sort of public disgrace (v. 39). He felt that he had let God down and let himself down. He may even have been in fear of attack because he prays three times for God to preserve his life (vv. 25, 37, 40).

You might think that, in such a state, the last thing he would have felt like doing was to get his Bible out! In fact it's the *first* thing he wants to do. Look how many times in this short section he refers to God's Word, his commands, his law, his decrees and his statutes. He knows that God's words are good (v. 39); they are life-giving and life-preserving (v. 40).

REFLECTION

Turn back for a moment to Psalm 19:7–10. How has God's Word had these positive, renewing effects in your life? (See also John 6:63).

READ Psalm 119:41–48

God's law and God's Word

God has spoken to humankind. That truth is not debated in the psalms; it is accepted and celebrated. God has spoken in creation. He has also spoken to us in the Law (Torah), prophets and writings, which together make up our Old Testament. He has spoken supremely in the person of Jesus Christ (Heb. 1:1–3) and through his appointed apostles and prophets in the New Testament Scriptures.

For the psalmists, writing in the first millennium before Christ, their 'Bible' was mainly the Torah, the first five books of our Old Testament. This contained the accounts of creation, God's calling of Abraham, the formation of God's people and their deliverance from slavery – much more than 'laws' as we use that term today. In John 10:34 Jesus said to the religious leaders of his day, 'Is it not written in your Law …?' and then quoted Psalm 82. Likewise, in the psalms 'your law' and 'your word' are sometimes interchangeable terms. So this psalmist exclaims, 'I trust in your word' (v. 42) and 'I will always obey your law' (v. 44; see also vv. 89, 97).

Like Psalm 19, this psalm uses several different words to help us understand the purpose and value of God's Word and its many different facets. There are laws (v. 43), precepts (v. 45) and statutes (v. 46). There are also commands and decrees (vv. 47–48), and promises (v. 41).

With due apology to any lawyers or historians, the thought of ploughing through ancient documents dating back some three thousand years is not one that excites most of us. But the psalmist loves God's word and finds it 'a delight' (v. 47). So he trusts in God's Word and sets himself to obey it (v. 44) and to share it boldly (v. 46). He also bases his hope on what God has promised: 'May your unfailing love come to me, LORD, according to your promise' (v. 41).

REFLECTION

As we read the Bible, let's pray, 'Open my eyes that I may see wonderful things in your law' (v. 18). Let's then turn what we learn into prayer, praise and responsive action.

Opposition

If you hold to the truth of the Bible, then expect opposition! That seems to be a constant in every generation and in every culture. It was certainly the experience of the psalmist. He refers to 'my suffering '(v. 50) and to being taunted, mocked, smeared and even taken captive:

- 'The arrogant mock me' (v. 51);

- 'the wicked bind me with ropes' (v. 61); and

- 'the arrogant smear me with lies' (v. 69).

We might think that such opposition would quickly undermine his faith, but it has the opposite effect. It seems to confirm him in his love for the Word of God and a desire to know God more (vv. 68–72). He knows that the Word of God has a powerful effect on his life:

- assuring him of God's grace (v. 58);

- showing him the right way to live (v. 59); and

- bringing him comfort and hope (vv. 49–50, 52).

As he reflects on the opposition he faces, and on his commitment to live in accordance with God's law, he prays:

- that he would experience more of God's 'unfailing love' (v. 41);

- for God to remember his promises (vv. 49, 58); and

- for God to 'Do good to your servant according to your word' (v. 65).

He makes commitments to remember the Word of God wherever he is (v. 54) and even at night (vv. 55, 62), and reaffirms what he truly values: God's Word is a delight and 'more precious to me than thousands of pieces of silver and gold' (v. 72).

Looking back on the struggle he has faced, both with his own sin and with the opposition from unbelievers, he reflects that this was part of God's work for good in his life: 'Before I was afflicted I went astray, but now I obey your word' (v. 67; see also v. 71 and Rom. 5:3–5).

REFLECTION

The real opposition faced by Christian believers in every generation is not from people, but from the powers of evil. What weapons does God provide for us to fight that battle? (Eph. 6:1–11).

Unrelenting pressure; unfailing love

The psalmist's problems continue. He is opposed by arrogant people (vv. 78, 85) and suffering persecution 'without cause' (vv. 78, 86). He feels 'like a wineskin in the smoke' (v. 83), presumably meaning that he is feeling dried out, emotionally, physically and spiritually. His soul 'faints with longing' (v. 81) for God to deliver him. He knows he has nothing left to give and feels close to giving up on God: 'My eyes fail, looking for your promise' (v. 82).

And yet … he knows that God has not given up on him. He reminds himself that God made him (v. 73), that God's laws are good and right (v. 75), and that his love will never fail (v. 76). So he asks God two questions:

1. 'When will you comfort me?' (v. 82); and

2. 'How long must your servant wait?' (v. 84).

We are not told how or when these questions were answered. We do know that while he waits, the psalmist continues to delight in God's Word (v. 77), which includes his commands (vv. 73, 86), laws (v. 75), precepts (vv. 78, 87), statutes (vv. 79, 88) and decrees (vv. 80, 83), and is clear in his resolve to understand and obey God's Word. His hope is in the Word of the Lord (v. 74) and in the Lord of the Word (v. 81).

It is while going through his very testing experience that the psalmist prays for understanding of God's Word (v. 73) and for the ability to 'wholeheartedly' live God's way (v. 80). He affirms his ongoing commitment to 'meditate on your precepts' (v. 78) and finds comfort in the unfailing love and compassion of God.

REFLECTION

Jesus never promised that life would be easy for the believer – rather the opposite (John 15:18; 16:33) – but in the midst of trouble we are promised that nothing 'will be able to separate us from the love of God that is in Christ Jesus our Lord' (Rom. 8:39). It is when we are in a desperate state, like this psalmist, that we prove for ourselves that our God is 'the Father of compassion and the God of all comfort' (2 Cor. 1:3).

Strong foundation; lasting security

Where do you hope to find security in a very uncertain world? Where do you look for a firm foundation when the ground seems to be moving under your feet and your particular world seems to be falling apart?

This psalmist finds delight and a deep sense of security in the knowledge that the God who created the world is the same God who gave his law and the same God who is faithful to the covenant of love he made with his people. God's word 'is eternal; it stands firm in the heavens' (v. 89), the world God created 'endures' (v. 90) and his 'faithfulness continues through all generations' (v. 90).

These great certainties provide the strongest possible foundation for life, and the greatest possible security, for every believer in every generation. When we human beings try to be far too smart for our own good – denying the Creator, ignoring God's Word and rejecting his love – we are left with a life with no strong foundation, without hope or purpose and with no answer to death.

Today's reading, like all of Psalm 119, focuses particularly on the Word of God, its eternal truth and its life-giving power. God's Word is a delight that keeps us through testing times (vv. 92–93), from much evil (v. 95) and from wandering away from God (v. 101). God's Word is perfect (v. 96). It is 'sweet' to taste (v. 103) – as good to read and study as honey is to eat (see also Ps. 19:10). When we read and meditate on God's Word and seek to live it out, we become wiser (vv. 98, 100), and so learn to love God and hate evil (v. 104).

REFLECTION

The Bible tells us that even the world God created will not last for ever. One day God will bring this world to an end (see 2 Pet. 3:10–11), but his Word will remain true for ever and his love will never end (Ps. 118:1). This is the foundation on which to build our lives (Matt. 7:24). This is the ultimate security. As Jesus said, 'Heaven and earth will pass away, my words will never pass away' (Mark 13:31).

 **DAY 25**

A lamp and a light

'Your word is a lamp for my feet, a light on my path' (v. 105).

Imagine walking down a lonely, dark path at night, looking for an unlit house somewhere ahead. You wish you had a torch in your hand to shine down at your feet, to stop you tripping over. Then a security light is switched on, illuminating the house and your path. Now you can see the way to your destination. God's Word is a light to us in both these senses. It shows where we are heading and the way we should go. It also keeps us from falling or wandering off the path.

When I first started reading the Bible as an adult in my early 20s, it was like a light being turned on in my life. It opened up a reality about the existence of God and the person of Jesus Christ that I had previously rejected. I realised that I had been groping around in the dark. Now, through the written Word, God was showing me the way to know him and the way he wanted me to live.

This psalmist wants a light and a lamp because he is committed to obeying God's law (vv. 101, 111–112), but he is under a lot of pressure to compromise and wander away from God (vv. 107, 109–110). He trusts in God and in his Word (v. 114), but his faith is being tested (vv. 123, 134). He feels threatened and tempted by the evil around him (v. 115).

So he asks God to sustain him and keep him in the face of pressure from arrogant people (vv. 121–122, 132–134). He longs for God to act (v. 120) because he is distressed at the way God's law is being openly disregarded (v. 136). He also knows in his own experience that: 'The unfolding of your words gives light' (v. 130).

REFLECTION

Jesus said, 'I am the light of the world. Whoever follows me will never walk in darkness, but will have the light of life' (John 8:12). What does it mean in practical terms to 'walk in the light' (1 John 1:7)?

Learning through difficulty

When I first became a Christian, I was told that to grow in my faith I needed to read the Bible, pray and join a church. It all sounded so simple! What I was not told, but what I have learned, is that we grow through hard experiences, disappointments and setbacks when our faith is tested. Sometimes it's in our most difficult experiences that we learn to value the promises and the presence of God.

The writer of this psalm shares his struggles with us. He is 'lowly and despised (v. 141). 'Trouble and distress have come upon me' (v. 143). He refers to 'my suffering' (v. 153) and being persecuted (vv. 157, 161).

But it's in the middle of these difficulties, when his faith is being tested, that he learns to value the promises of God: to love the Word of God (v. 140) and take delight in it (v. 143). The characteristics of God are now much more than just intellectual beliefs or words to recite in a creed. He has come to know God for himself through proving God's promises and experiencing God's presence in tough situations:

- in an evil world he values God's righteousness (vv. 137–138);

- in a dangerous situation he is thankful for God's rescue (v. 154);

- in a world of lies, spin and propaganda he has learned to love the truth of God's Word (vv. 160, 163); and

- in desperate need he is thankful that God still loves him and hears his prayers (vv. 145–149).

So he prays for even greater understanding (v. 169) and for the Lord to put a song of praise in his heart (vv. 171–172).

REFLECTION

In the last two verses the psalmist shares his very human struggle of faith. Like us perhaps, he is conscious of the flaws in his character that lead him to wander away from God's path. So he appeals to the Lord as his shepherd to come looking for him and find him (v. 176; see also Luke 15:3–7; John 10:11–15). For his part he will keep focused on God and his Word for daily wisdom and strength (vv. 175–176).

 **DAY 27**

Pilgrims on a journey

In the next 15 psalms we join the pilgrims traveling from the surrounding areas up to Jerusalem to celebrate one of the great feasts (Deut. 16:16). This psalm is the first of the 'songs of ascent' (Ps. 120–134), traditionally sung by the pilgrims on their journey.

The author of this psalm is bemoaning the fact that he is exiled from the land of Israel. He is an expatriate, longingly looking back towards home. Meshek in the north and Kedar in the south (v. 5) represent, poetically, lands far away from home. He laments, 'Too long have I lived among those who hate peace' (v. 6). He has had enough of living with deceit and lies (v. 2), perhaps not least the deceitfulness of sin in his own heart. He is worn down with the tension of being a man of peace in a violent society (v. 7). So he cries out in distress to the Lord for help (v. 1).

The New Testament helps us understand this psalm. We journey towards heaven, the way is difficult, but we are heading to our true home: 'our citizenship is in heaven' (Phil. 3:20). In the meantime we are foreigners and exiles (1 Pet. 2:11–12), pilgrims on a journey, each day needing to 'pitch my moving tent a day's march nearer home'.[2] God puts into the heart of every believer thankfulness for all the good things to be enjoyed on earth, but also a longing to be 'with Christ, which is better by far' (Phil. 1:23; see also 2 Cor. 4:16 – 5:5).

REFLECTION

We journey every day towards heaven. In the meantime God still has work for us to do in service of him. Like this psalmist we may get depressed and overcome by all the evil in the world, but God does not leave us. Like the psalmist we can still call out to God in our distress and rely on him for help.

God's keeping power

Who do we look to for help when we are in trouble? Most likely we look to family and friends for support. Beyond that, secular western culture tells us to look *within ourselves* for the resources to face our problems and overcome them. The psalms, like the whole Bible, give us a completely different world view. There is a God who made us. We were never meant to journey through life without him.

Widely known as 'the traveller's psalm', this is a song for pilgrims. Conscious of all the threats and dangers on their journey, they nevertheless look to the Lord to protect them and bring them safely to their destination. We can picture the writer, travelling up to Jerusalem and looking up to the hills (v. 1), perhaps for inspiration or perhaps in fear of bandits. Then, remembering the Lord who made the hills, he affirms, 'My help comes from the LORD, the Maker of heaven and earth' (v. 2). This is the key verse of this psalm: a clear statement of faith. The traveller is feeling vulnerable and conscious of danger on his journey, and looks to God for help.

Like many of the psalms, the focus of attention shifts as it progresses: from 'I' and 'my' (vv. 1–2) to 'your' singular (v. 3), to the whole people of God (v. 4) and back to the individual believer (vv. 5–8). So he encourages his fellow believers, 'He will not let *your* foot slip – he who watches over *you* will not slumber' (v. 3, my italics), a promise repeated as he pictures the threats from the burning sun by day, and the night with its darkness and fears (vv. 4–6). The psalmist concludes, 'The LORD ... will watch over *your* life' (v. 7). This means all of your life – spiritual and material, work and home, worship and prayer, success and failure, good times and bad.

REFLECTION

Our circumstances and moods change, our location on God's earth changes as we move around for work or leisure, but God's presence and keeping power and love will never change and never end (v. 8). This psalm encourages us to entrust ourselves to him.

DAY 29

'Pray for the peace of Jerusalem'

In this psalm the pilgrims have now arrived at Jerusalem: verses 1–2 express the joy of arriving; verses 3–5 the unity of God's people; and verses 6–9 a vision of peace.

For the psalmist, Jerusalem was the great city, the place where the whole people of God gathered (v. 4) to praise him according to the statute which required that the people only sacrifice in places the Lord had designated (Deut. 12:13). Jerusalem was the place where God had set his name (1 Kgs. 11:36) and where David had ruled as king. That's why they prayed, 'For the sake of the house of the LORD our God, I will seek your prosperity' (v. 9).

But without the presence of the Lord himself, Jerusalem was just another city with religious shrines and relics. Ezekiel saw in a vision the glory of the Lord leaving the temple because the people had turned their backs on him (Ezek. 9–10). More than that, the city was under God's judgement because of the evil done by its leaders (Ezek. 11:2), its unnecessary violence (Ezek. 11:6) and its people turning away from God (Ezek. 11:12). So the city's divine protection was removed and the city was destroyed by the Babylonians in 587 BC. In his time Jesus wept over Jerusalem because the people had rejected God's Messiah. Jesus foresaw not peace but violence and the destruction of the city, which came in AD 70 (Luke 13:34; 19:41–45; John 11:48).

REFLECTION

How are we to understand the love of the 'house of the LORD' and love for the city of Jerusalem expressed in this psalm? According to the New Testament, the 'house of God' is no longer the temple. It is the people of God gathered together. So, as the Israelites expressed their love for Jerusalem, Christians express love for the church not as a building, institution or organisation, but as the worldwide community of people professing faith in Jesus Christ. As the psalmist prayed for the peace of Jerusalem, so Christians are called to pray and work for the growth of the church because it is 'a dwelling in which God lives by his Spirit' (Eph. 2:22). Like pilgrims, we travel, but towards heaven rather than to any earthly city (Heb. 12:22–24; 13:14).

Eyes on the Lord

What do we mean when we say, 'I looked to them for help'? Or, 'I look to them for support in this situation'? To 'look' to someone usually means that we *rely* on them, and we rely on that particular person because we *know* them and have good reason to trust that they will not let us down.

Here the psalmist looks to the Lord for help: 'I lift up my eyes to you, to you who sit enthroned in heaven' (v. 1). He looks to the Lord because he knows the Lord, and knows that he can rely on the Lord for help. Like in Psalm 121, he knows, 'My help comes from the LORD, the Maker of heaven and earth' (Ps. 121:2). But here he is looking for mercy (vv. 2–3) – for God to take pity on Israel, to take ownership of the problem which his people were facing and to rescue them. He pictures the way a servant looks to their boss for direction, support and relief (v. 2).

He looks to the Lord for mercy because the people are suffering contempt and ridicule from proud and arrogant people. He has suffered enough and he knows the people he is so concerned about can't take much more: 'we have endured *no end of* contempt. We have endured *no end of* ridicule from the arrogant, of contempt from the proud' (vv. 3–4, my italics).

Sometimes this dismissive, aggressive, malicious contempt, which Jesus himself suffered, is particularly hard to bear (Lam. 3:30, 33). Wisely the psalmist doesn't try to summon up the strength to keep going from within himself. No, his eyes are on the Lord, whose throne is in heaven (v. 1) and who is the one ultimately in charge (v. 2).

REFLECTION

When you feel you have simply had enough and can't face any more, make this very simple prayer in verses 1–2 your own. God will surely answer.

'If the LORD had not been on our side ...'

I wonder how many of God's people over the last three millennia have echoed the sentiment of the opening words of this psalm: 'If the LORD had not been on our side ...' (v. 1)? Or, 'If God had not helped me, I would not have come through that ordeal'?

This fifth 'song of ascent' looks back to a dangerous, threatening attack on the land of Israel from one of Israel's enemies in the time of David (see 2 Sam. 5:17–25). This attack by the Philistines was much more than just another harassing raid; it was meant to put an end to David's kingdom.

The psalmist states, 'If the LORD had not been on our side ... when people attacked us, they would have swallowed us alive' (vv. 1–3); or, to change the metaphor, 'the flood would have engulfed us' (v. 4). They would have drowned in the tsunami-like wave that hit them (vv. 4–5). The psalmist changes the metaphor again to picture his enemies like wild animals and he praises the Lord 'who has not let us be torn by their teeth' (v. 6). Then he pictures his foes like hunters from whom they had escaped 'like a bird from the fowler's snare' (v. 7). How did they escape? It was because the Lord helped them. The surrounding tribes worshipped different 'local' gods. But David sees that their deliverance was from 'the LORD, the Maker of heaven and earth' (v. 8).

REFLECTION

Think back on your own times of struggle and remember with thankfulness, 'If it had not been for the LORD ...' Think about the church worldwide, persecuted and struggling, and remember with thankfulness, 'If it had not been for the LORD ...' As we look forward, let's also remember with confidence, 'Our help is in the name of the LORD, the Maker of heaven and earth' (v. 8). As Israel looked back to deliverance from their enemies, we look back to a greater deliverance – from sin, death and hell – by our Lord Jesus Christ when he died and rose again (Col. 1:13–14). Praise God!

'Those who trust in the LORD'

To say 'I believe in God' might be just a concept discussed with friends over a coffee. This psalm, though, restates the biblical truth that faith goes much deeper than mere intellectual belief. It involves orienting our whole life towards God, relying on God, and believing and receiving God's Word. Our trust in the unseen God and in his revealed truth will always be tested in this world by the ever present reality of evil. But 'Those who trust in the LORD … cannot be shaken' (v. 1). True faith means to trust God's Word and to trust God himself.

The psalm paints a picture of total security for the believer: 'As the mountains surround Jerusalem, so the LORD surrounds his people' (v. 2). Who are his people? It is those who trust in him. Jesus underlined the truth that Abraham's real descendants are not those who can trace their ancestry back to Abraham but those who had faith like Abraham (John 8:39). The Apostle Paul, who, like Jesus, was born into a Jewish society, underlined this principle further in his letter to the Romans (Rom. 4:11–12; 9:6–8).

The psalmist longs, as we might in our generation, for a society at peace: a just society where good is rewarded and honoured, and where evil is hated and punished (vv. 4–5). We look forward to the day when God winds up history, when Jesus returns and when he establishes his kingdom of justice and peace. In the meantime, we have a foretaste of that peace because of the sacrifice of Jesus: 'we have peace with God through our Lord Jesus Christ' (Rom. 5:1). We are called to share that good news with others (2 Cor. 5:18–21).

REFLECTION

In this very uncertain world, this psalm reminds us that our only lasting security is in the Lord himself (v. 1). The New Testament encourages us to pray in every situation and, as we do, promises, 'the peace of God, which transcends all understanding, will guard your hearts and your minds in Christ Jesus' (Phil. 4:7).

God's work and ours

In the spread of the Christian gospel, and in building his church, God uses the same principles of sowing and reaping that he built into the world he created. We work in breaking up the ground, sowing, nurturing and harvesting, but none of it would be any use unless God gives life and growth (1 Cor. 3:6–7).

What God does (vv. 1–3)

The psalmist is thankful for God's work in the past. Times had been good. The Lord had 'restored the fortunes of Zion' (v. 1), most likely a reference to Israel's return from the years of captivity in Babylon. It was like a wonderful dream; something they had longed for had finally come to pass. They were back in their homeland. There was laughter and joy, singing and celebration (v. 2). Even the surrounding nations saw God's hand at work in restoring the nation of Israel. The people themselves looked back with thankfulness: 'The LORD has done great things for us, and we are filled with joy' (v. 3).

What we do (vv. 4–6)

But the good times were in the past and life is now hard, with little sign of God at work (v. 4). How do the people respond? They continue with the hard work of sowing (v. 5). They weep because of the hard state of the ground, but they press on, trusting God's promise that spreading the seed will result in a harvest and will be a cause to celebrate (v. 6).

They not only work; they pray. The psalmist prays, 'Restore our fortunes, LORD, like streams in the Negev' (that is, the desert, v. 4). This is a prayer for God to work, doing now what he had done in the past.

REFLECTION

God works as he wills. But our job is clear: to pray and spread the Word of God by whatever means we can. This is the work to which every believer is called, in every generation and in every culture. The harvest is then up to the Lord. Jesus made this clear in his parable of the sower (Matt. 13:1-23).

All in vain

Trust in God isn't just a matter for Sundays; it's a way of life. This psalm reminds us to trust God for guidance and help in every area of life, home, work, leisure and family. Added together, these activities take up most of our waking hours. Finding, building or renting a home; working to make a living; raising a family; keeping ourselves and our families safe – these all absorb most of our time and energy. Psalm 127 reminds us that without God, all our efforts are ultimately pointless.

You may have noticed that each of these short 'songs of ascent' contains a single, powerful, simple idea. For example:

Psalm 120   calling on the Lord for help;

Psalm 121   God's keeping power;

Psalm 122   peace;

Psalm 123   looking to the Lord;

Psalm 124   God's rescue from danger;

Psalm 125   trusting in the Lord; and

Psalm 126   restoration.

Psalm 127 makes the very simple point that without God, nothing in life makes sense or has purpose or will ultimately prove successful. It is a theme developed with penetrating wisdom and insight in the Old Testament book of Ecclesiastes. This psalm reminds us that without God at the centre of it all, our efforts will be 'in vain'. The outcomes we strive so hard to achieve, the happiness we seek, the business success we strive for, even our family life will ultimately be meaningless

The psalm puts it like this:

- 'Unless the LORD builds the house, the builders labour in vain' (v. 1);

- 'Unless the LORD watches over the city, the guards stand watch in vain' (v. 1);

- Unless God is at the centre of our life, all our hard work and late nights are 'in vain' (v. 2); and

- 'Children are a heritage from the LORD': if we are blessed with children, then let us value them as precious gifts from God entrusted to our care (vv. 4–6).

REFLECTION

Commit all your life – work, family, home, security – to the Lord and trust him with it: 'Trust in the LORD with all your heart … In all your ways submit to him, and he will make your paths straight' (Prov. 3:5–6).

The blessings of family

Families are a blessing from the Lord. They are also the building blocks of any stable society. In Psalm 127 we were reminded of the great blessing of children. This psalm builds on that theme and paints an ideal picture of family life, in the same way that Psalms 1 and 15 portray an individual life lived well under God.

The blessing of God is for those who 'fear' him (vv. 1, 4) – who honour, respect and obey him. The blessing promised here is of fruitful, productive, fulfilling work (v. 2), and of a strong marriage and family life (v. 3). Notice how the psalm progressively expands its focus, from the individual believer (vv. 1–2) to the family circle (vv. 3–4), to the city (v. 5) and finally to the nation (v. 6).

With the picture of this blessed life comes a prayer with four specific requests:

- 'May the LORD bless you' (v. 5);

- 'may you see the prosperity of Jerusalem' (v. 5);

- 'May you live to see your children's children' (v. 6); and

- may peace be upon God's people (v. 6).

Proverbs reminds us that the 'fear of the LORD' is the beginning of knowledge and wisdom (Prov. 1:7; 9:10). This fear of God is not a fear of punishment or of an unpredictable boss, but of love and respect and a desire to honour the one who has been so good to us.

REFLECTION

This is truly the foundation of a blessed life. If we dispense with God, live only to please ourselves and ignore our Maker's instructions for life, then we shouldn't be surprised if we reap what we sow. When marriages fall apart and when family life becomes a battleground of arguments, abuse and violence, then people get hurt and our society itself starts to breakdown. By contrast, as we are reminded in the psalms, honouring God with our whole life is the best way to live. It's the way our loving God intends us to live.

Oppressed, but not defeated

Sadly there are many who can echo the opening words of this psalm: 'They have greatly oppressed me from my youth' (v. 1) – like my Sudanese friend growing up in a war-torn country; or the victims of child abuse; and so many young people who are exploited or bullied, either physically or via social media or both. Bad experiences in childhood leave scars which never fully heal. But with the Lord there is always hope, and we find that hope in verse 2: 'but they have not gained the victory over me.' The psalmist prays in verses 5–8 for those who oppose God: 'May they be like grass on the roof, which withers before it can grow' (v. 6). Such grass is quickly burned up in the hot weather. It has no roots, and no substance or lasting value.

The picture of childhood in this psalm seems to apply to Israel as a nation rather than to an individual. Israel is referred to in Scripture as God's son, called 'out of Egypt' (Hos. 11:1). Certainly Israel as a nation had a traumatic and difficult 'childhood'. After the Lord delivered them from slavery in Egypt, the people wandered for 40 years in the desert, learning hard lessons the hard way, grumbling, disobeying and being disciplined (v. 3).

The psalm also applies to Jesus, the true Israel, who was taken to Egypt as a child, and in whom this prophecy was fulfilled (Matt. 2:15). As a man he was tested in a wilderness experience (Matt. 4:1-11), but, unlike Israel, he did not fail.

REFLECTION

Our Lord Jesus Christ was oppressed, but not defeated. He died on a cross, but God raised him from the dead. God has promised that whatever oppression we may have to suffer cannot defeat us because nothing 'will be able to separate us from the love of God that is in Christ Jesus our Lord' (Rom. 8:39; see also Rom. 8:17, 28–38).

 **DAY 37**

Praying, waiting and hoping

The opening line, 'Out of the depths I cry to you, LORD', may sound familiar. It reads like many of the psalms of David in Book 1. What deep hole is the writer in this time? Here it is not doubt, depression or attack from enemies, but rather a conviction of his own sinfulness.

Praying (vv. 1–4)

The psalmist asks for mercy. Why? Because he remembers that if the Lord kept a record of our sins, we would have no hope (v. 3) 'But', as verse 4 continues, with the Lord there is forgiveness, a restored relationship and the opportunity to live a useful, fulfilling life in God's service.

Waiting (vv. 5–6)

He writes, 'I wait for the LORD' (v. 5). He's not just wanting forgiveness and relief from guilt, but longing for the Lord himself. How does he wait? He relies on the Word of God (v. 5). He looks to God to speak through his Word, and waits patiently and longingly for God to fulfil his promises. He waits 'more than watchmen wait for the morning' (v. 6). For the night watchman, the night may seem never ending, but morning eventually comes. The sun rises, the night ends and a new day begins.

Hoping (vv. 7–8)

Hoping is not wishful thinking; it is waiting expectantly for God's promises to be fulfilled. The outcome is certain. It is the waiting that's hard. But just as the psalmist's hope is in God's Word, so he calls all God's people to put their hope in the Lord because of his unfailing love (v. 7). He will redeem us from our sins (vv. 7–8). In Jesus Christ he paid the ransom price (Mark 10:45).

As he prays and waits, he finds a solid ground for his future hope: his assurance of God's love. He started in 'the depths' (v. 1), but he finishes on a high. What a contrast! What makes the difference? He knows he has been forgiven, redeemed and loved by God. That experience and knowledge is transformational.

REFLECTION

How has knowing that God loves you, and forgiven your sin through Jesus Christ, changed your life? Read 1 John 4:7–12.

Contentment

'I am content!' How many of us can say that? How often could we say it with honesty? I have a book at home by the seventeenth-century Puritan Jeremiah Burroughs called *The Rare jewel of Christian Contentment*. It's a rare jewel indeed because most of us spend our lives in a state of anxious worry and discontent.

This psalm paints a beautiful picture of contentment – of being at peace with oneself, with God and with the world: 'But I have calmed and quietened myself, I am like a weaned child with its mother' (v. 2). If you are a stressed-out parent with demanding children, finding it hard to relate to that idyllic scene, picture perhaps those precious times when your child is behaving particular well or cuddling up to you on the sofa at the end of a long day. In that moment they are content, and so are you.

So what is the secret of contentment? It is humility, thankfulness and most of all the priceless peace of mind and sense of rightness that comes from being close to Christ. The psalm opens, 'My heart is not proud, LORD, my eyes are not haughty'. This is not about low self-esteem or dodging responsibility; it is about not undervaluing others and not presuming to overvalue oneself (see Rom. 12:3, 16). No wonder, having experienced God's peace for himself, David urges God's people, 'put your hope in the LORD' (v. 3) and so find this peace for themselves.

The Apostle Paul had learned to be 'content' even while in prison (Phil. 4:12). He didn't learn that from a book or from a lifestyle seminar. He learned it through the hard knocks of experience when he had suffered various wants and deprivations. Paul knew what he was talking about when he encouraged Timothy to be content with what he had and not long for more (1 Tim. 6:6–9).

REFLECTION

What causes discontentment in your life? What can you learn from David's experience of finding contentment?

God's promises and God's presence

The events of 2 Samuel 7 form the background to this psalm. David had promised to build a 'house' for God, that is, a temple, but God promised to build David a 'house', meaning a lasting dynasty. This promise was fulfilled in the coming of Jesus, God's Messiah, who was both David's descendant, humanly speaking, and the unique Son of God (Rom. 1:3).

The psalm is in two parts: David's promise to God and God's promise to David. It begins with David's well-intentioned commitment, and ends with the glory and victory of the promised Messiah (vv. 17–18), characterised by strength (the horn), light (the lamp) and authority (the crown).

David's promise to God (vv. 1–9)

The psalm celebrates the bringing of the ark of God, the symbol of God's presence, to Jerusalem. The psalmist calls on the Lord to remember David's promise and commitment in making this happen (2 Sam. 6:1–2).

God's promise to David (vv. 10–18)

The psalmist calls on God to 'remember' his covenant to David. It isn't that the Lord has somehow forgotten. Rather it's a plea for God to deliver on the commitments he has made in the past. The Lord had chosen Zion (Jerusalem) as his dwelling place (vv. 13–14) and had promised to bless the people (vv. 15–16).

The Old Testament tells us how the people misunderstood and took this promise for granted. In Jeremiah's day they thought that the mere presence of the temple guaranteed their safety, so it didn't matter how they lived (Jer. 7:1–7). That illusion was shattered when the Babylonians destroyed the city and the people went into slavery.

In Jesus' day the rebuilt temple had become a great money-making scam, where would-be worshippers were financially exploited by the religious authorities (Matt. 21:13). No wonder it made Jesus so angry. The outcome? Their temple was again destroyed, this time by the Romans, never to be rebuilt.

REFLECTION

We look forward to the fulfilment of this psalm when Jesus returns in glory. In the meantime, we have the promise of God's presence with us, a privilege to be enjoyed, but never to be taken lightly.

Unity, harmony and blessing

Today we have two short psalms: the first about the blessing of unity; the second about praising and blessing God.

Unity (Ps. 133)

Proximity does not gurantee unity. Some families live in the same town and neighbourhood, but barely speak to each other. Others can be spread across the world, but keep very strong bonds of love and support. Yet how good it is to be with those you love!

This psalm gives us two pictures of God blessing his people with unity. The first is of oil flowing down the priestly figure of Aaron, Moses' brother (v. 2). The second is of God making dew to fall, not on the high mountains of Hermon, which would be expected, but on the low-level 'Mount Zion' in Jerusalem, the place where the Lord had set his name (v. 3). Both pictures remind us that every good blessing in this life comes down from above (Jas. 1:17). Unity is one of the Lord's most valuable blessings.

In the family of God we have a God-given unity through belonging to Jesus Christ. We have a bond with fellow believers no matter what our gender, race, colour, age, education level or status in society: we 'are all one in Christ Jesus' (Gal. 3:28). But because we remain sinful, self-centred people, we have to work hard on our relationships to maintain and build that unity (Eph. 4:3).

Unity is strength. Where there is unity in a family or church, 'there the LORD bestows his blessing, even life for evermore' (v. 3).

Blessing (Ps. 134)

This last of the 'songs of ascents' celebrates the pilgrims' arrival at the temple at the end of their journey. It is full of praise and thanksgiving. It begins with the people praising or blessing the Lord (v. 1), and ends by asking the Lord to bless his people (v. 3). When we bless God, we praise and thank him. When God blesses us, he gives us that deep sense of belonging, of being right with him, that only comes from being at peace with him (see John 14:27).

REFLECTION

What are your best experiences of Christian worship, fellowship and service together with others? What has made those experiences so special and memorable?

Praise the name of the Lord

As we read Psalm 135, we find some phrases which might sound familiar. That's because several verses also appear in other psalms (notably Psalms 115 and 136). But this psalm stands by itself in calling us to praise our God.

We are called to 'Praise the LORD' and to 'Praise the name of the LORD' (v. 1). Why is so much emphasis put on the name of God, in psalms and throughout the whole Bible? It's because Yahweh (or 'the LORD') is the personal name of God revealed to Israel. It is a statement of his *character*: holy, just, good, loving and everlasting. The name of the Lord also reminds them of the *covenant* God made with Abraham, Isaac and Jacob and of his promise to be faithful to those covenant promises – to be their God for ever (v. 13).

His name is to be praised because:

- he is good (v. 3). His name is good (Ps. 52:9) and praising him is good (v. 3; Ps. 147:1)

- he has chosen Jacob, later renamed Israel (v. 4). God in his grace chose a man with many obvious flaws to be the 'father' of his people. It was to Jacob's descendants that he gave his law, to them he sent his prophets and to them he sent his Son to be the Saviour for the whole world.

- he is the Creator (vv. 6–7) who delivered his people from slavery in Egypt with miraculous acts (vv. 8–9), gave them victory over their enemies and brought them into the land he promised them (vv. 10–12).

- he will vindicate his people when they are mocked and persecuted (v. 14).

- he is greater than idols or any other gods which people worship (vv. 5, 15–18; see also Ps. 115:4–8).

So the whole nation, the priests and all who fear the Lord are called to praise him (vv. 19–21).

REFLECTION

The same honour given to the name 'Yahweh' in this psalm is reserved for the name of Jesus in the New Testament. His is 'the name that is above every name' (Phil. 2:9), because he is God's revelation of himself in human form, our Lord and our Saviour (Phil. 2:11).

God's enduring love

Consider these three questions:

1. What is of lasting value in a fast-changing world?

2. Where is security to be found in an uncertain world?

3. Who, or what, can we rely on when people let us down?

The Bible's answer to all three questions is God's unchanging, steadfast love. At first sight that may sound over-simplistic, or even sentimental, but it is deeply profound. The Apostle Paul realised that even the best minds needed God-given insight and wisdom to understand 'how wide and long and high and deep is the love of Christ' (Eph. 3:18). So he prayed that we might know and experience for ourselves that love 'that surpasses knowledge' (Eph. 3:19).

This is an antiphonal psalm with 26 verses. The first line of each verse was most probably sung by a worship leader, with the congregation singing (or saying) the second line in response. That responsive chorus is repeated 25 times so we get the clear message: 'His love endures for ever' (see also Ps. 118:1–4).

As we consider these words about the love of God, we might ask a fourth question: how do we *know* God loves us? The Bible's answer is that we know because of what he has done for us: 'God so loved the word that he gave his one and only Son' (John 3:16).

This psalm celebrates:

- the greatness of God (vv. 1–4);
- what he has done in creation (vv. 5–9); and
- what he has done in redeeming his people, delivering them from slavery in Egypt and across the Red Sea (vv. 10–15), guiding them through the wilderness (v. 16), giving them victory over their enemies (vv. 17–20, 23–24) and establishing them in their own land (vv. 21–22).

The scope of thanksgiving widens as the psalmist remembers that God's providential care extends way beyond the Israelites: 'He gives food to every creature' (v. 25). So he concludes, 'Give thanks to the God of heaven. His love endures for ever' (v. 26).

REFLECTION

The New Testament encourages us to look back and recall what God has done in Jesus Christ to demonstrate his love for us (Rom. 5:8). It also reminds us that nothing can 'separate us from the love of God that is in Christ Jesus our Lord' (Rom. 8:38).

Songs from a strange land

What are we to make of this psalm? It's at the other end of the spectrum to the uplifting songs of praise or comforting prayers that we may prefer to turn to in the psalms.

It's a song from people in captivity, longing to be back in Jerusalem (vv. 1, 5–6). Their city had been violently destroyed by a powerful invading army. They had been taunted by their traditional enemies, the Edomites, who applauded as the Babylonians ripped Jerusalem apart brick by brick (v. 7). They had experienced the trauma of the ultimate war atrocity: their children being brutally killed (vv. 8–9). Now, to rub salt into the wound, their captors mockingly invite them to sing songs from their homeland to entertain them (vv. 2–3).

It's in that situation that they cry out for justice and vengeance. We naturally and rightly recoil from verses 8 and 9. It seems to express a desire for the Babylonians to suffer themselves what they had inflicted on others. But it is in accord with the Old Testament principle of exact retribution (Deut. 19:19). The offender was to suffer the same, not more and not less, than the harm they had inflicted on their victims.

This psalm is a cry from the heart for people who have suffered a great deal. Let us not be surprised, therefore, that it expresses a very human longing to pay enemies back for hurts and wrongs. After all, we are invited to 'pour out [our] hearts' to God (Ps. 62:8). But when Jesus suffered, he gave us an example of entrusting ourselves 'to him who judges justly' (1 Pet. 2:23), so we should imitate him.

REFLECTION

Perhaps the final word on this matter of whether or not to demand retribution is in Paul's letter to the Romans: 'Do not repay anyone evil for evil ... Do not take revenge, my dear friends, but leave room for God's wrath, for it is written: "It is mine to avenge; I will repay," says the Lord ... Do not be overcome by evil, but overcome evil with good (Rom. 12:17, 19, 21).

Boldness and humility

This is the first of a series of eight psalms of David that are included in this last of the five books that make up the collection of 150 psalms we have in the Bible.

A personal stand (vv. 1–3)

David commits to praising God with all his heart and to do so with a mix of boldness and humility.

He is bold in the face of other ideologies, world views and demonic powers: the other 'gods' worshipped in the cultures around him (v. 1). But he is humble in bowing down to worship the Lord and in praising his name because he knows that he is dependent on God's love and faithfulness every day he lives (v. 2). He is thankful that God has answered his prayer for help and strengthened him to face his challenges: 'you greatly emboldened me' (v. 3).

A global view (vv. 4–6)

David's faith is personal, but it is not private. He is unafraid to make his strong personal faith known in public. He has never thought of it as a belief system that is just true for him and should never be spoken about for fear of offending others. His faith is good news that has to be shared.

He prays for all the kings of the earth, as we are encouraged to do (1 Tim. 2:1–4). He wants all the world leaders to hear God's Word and to come to know for themselves that God is great (vv. 4–5). Yet he also cares for 'the lowly' (v. 6), those without power or influence who battle with life's problems.

A closing testimony (vv. 7–8)

David returns to his situation and to his personal faith. He is going through hard times, but remembers thankfully that God has preserved his life and rescued him from his enemies (v. 7).

He adds two short statements:

- 'The LORD will vindicate me' (v. 8); and

- 'your love, LORD, endures for ever' (v. 8).

He then ends with a prayer: 'do not abandon the works of your hands' (v. 8), in other words, 'do not leave us'.

REFLECTION

Let's pray for the same godly mix of boldness and humility in sharing our faith that we see in this psalm (see also 1 Pet. 3:15).

God knows us

We are known by God

God knows all about our physical, mental and spiritual condition. He knows what we do and even what we think (v. 2). He knows where we go and what we are about to say even before we speak it (vv. 3–4). He knows every thought, word, action and motive, and his knowledge of us is complete. How do we react to that? David, perhaps surprisingly, doesn't try to hide, like Adam and Eve did in the Garden of Eden (Gen. 3:8). Rather, he responds with amazement that God should know us so well (v. 6), and yet never leaves us (v. 7).

We were created by God

We are not the chance result of a random combination of chemicals and physical forces; we are God's creations: 'you created my inmost being; you knit me together in my mother's womb' (v. 13). David reflects with wonder that 'all the days ordained for me were written in your book before one of them came to be' (v. 16). When we grasp this truth, like David, we will want to praise God (v. 14).

We are sinful

After reflecting on the greatness of God and the miracle of human life, David looks around at the world and gets angry about its cruelty and injustice (vv. 19–22). But then he starts to recognise the problem of evil in himself and he ends on a note of sober realism, asking God to search his heart (vv. 23–24).

REFLECTION

How can we understand ourselves? Who can unravel the complex web of our thoughts, motives and instincts? Who can really explain how we are wired? We can find great relief and peace in knowing that there is a God who made us, loves us and wants us to know him. Wherever we go on God's earth, 'even there your hand will guide me, your right hand will hold me fast' (v. 10). It's the same security that Jesus promised all who follow him: 'I give them eternal life and they shall never perish; no one will snatch them out of my hand' (John 10:28).

Deliver us from evil

David's prayer for himself (vv. 1–5)

Sometimes evil is manifested in a love of cruelty and violence for its own sake. There may be no rational basis or just cause for it, only evil. So David prays to the Lord, whose power is greater than all, to rescue him from evildoers, to protect him from violent people and to keep him safe (vv. 1, 4). Their evil is shown in their hearts (v, 2), their tongues (v. 3), their hands (v. 4) and their arrogance (v. 5).

Confident faith (vv. 6–7)

In this dire situation David affirms his trust in the sovereign Lord: his God, his shield and his strong deliverer.

A prayer about the wicked (vv. 8–11)

David then prays that God would not allow the plans of these evil people to succeed (v. 8), but that they would experience a taste of their own medicine (vv. 9–11).

Assurance about God's justice (vv. 12–13)

Having committed all this to God in prayer, David moves forward, delighting in the certainty that God will execute justice on this earth (v. 12) and that the righteous will live to praise God and enjoy his presence (v. 13). He feels like a heavy load has been lifted from his back.

The prayers of Jesus

Jesus knew that evil would be an ever-present reality and threat to God's people until the end of time on this earth. When he taught his followers how to pray, he told them to pray daily for deliverance from evil (Matt. 6:13). He prayed for his followers that his Father would protect them (John 17:11) and specifically protect them from 'the evil one' (John 17:15).

> ## REFLECTION
>
> *Like Jesus, David experienced repeated onslaughts of evil and had his life threatened by evil people who accused him falsely and pursued him with malicious personal intent. This psalm is a great gift to believers in every generation who are under attack because it helps us to look to the Lord for deliverance and justice, and to remind ourselves that this is an experience Jesus himself went through for us to the maximum degree.*

Knowing our weaknesses

Here David asks God to hear his prayer and come quickly to help him (v. 1). He asks that his prayer will be as acceptable to God as any formal temple worship with its incense and evening sacrifice (v. 2).

David wants consistency and wholeness in his life. He is aware of his own fallibility and tendency to compromise with evil. He knows how easily he can take his eyes of faith away from the Lord. He is very conscious too of the presence of evil in the world and the many traps and pitfalls that he needs to avoid.

So he prays for God to help him in what he says (v. 3) and what he desires (v. 4). He is open to the direction and correction of good and wise people (v. 5). He wants to listen and learn. He particularly prays that that his eyes will remain steadfastly on the Lord (v. 8) and that God will help him navigate his way through life (vv. 9–10).

We have much to learn here about:

- what we say (v. 3). In words reminiscent of Proverbs 4:23–24, David asks God to 'guard his mouth' – to keep him from saying stupid or harmful words to others (see also Jas. 3:9–10).

- what we long for (v. 4). Knowing the sinfulness and deceitfulness of his own heart, and how easily he is led to do the wrong thing, David prays, 'Do not let my heart be drawn to what is evil'.

- where we look for guidance and inspiration (v. 8). Surrounded by evildoers, David proclaims, 'my eyes are fixed on you, Sovereign LORD'.

- where we 'walk' (that is, how we live, v. 9). David pictures himself walking along a path with many traps and snares, like walking through a minefield. So he prays, 'Keep me safe from the traps set by evildoers'.

REFLECTION

As we reflect on the temptations and decisions we face, on our weaknesses and on the way we can either help or hurt by the words we speak, this psalm is a good prayer for every day. Let's ask God to guard our mouth, our heart and our steps and to keep our eyes on him. See Hebrews 12:1–2.

Alone and needing help

David is in deep trouble and calling desperately on God for help. The header tells us he wrote this psalm while hiding in the cave from King Saul who was out to kill him (see 1 Sam. 24). It therefore reads like a pair with Psalm 57, which was written in the same situation. He is pursued by enemies and, not surprisingly, is at a very low point. His spirit is 'faint' (v. 3)

David feels totally alone (v. 4) and in 'desperate need' (v. 6). He was a strong military man who had fearlessly faced Goliath on his own, but here he acknowledges that his enemies are too strong for him. They are crushing him and he feels trapped in a personal hell (vv. 6–7). In this life-threatening situation he prays for God's mercy (v. 1).

This is a prayer of someone desperately needing God's help. It is very emotional. David *cries* out to the Lord (vv. 1, 5–6). He begs for God's rescue: 'I lift up my voice to the LORD for mercy' (v. 1). He unashamedly shouts out his prayers to God and holds nothing back: 'I pour out before him my complaint' (v. 2). He tells God all his trouble. Yet it ends with David longing for deliverance from his situation so that he can again praise God in such a way that others will see the goodness of God in his life and join him in faith and praise (v. 7).

David feels alone humanly speaking, but he is still trusting in his God and still talks confidently to the Lord in prayer: 'When my spirit grows faint within me, it is you who watch over my way' (v. 3) ... 'You are my refuge, my portion in the land of the living' (v. 5). He is still confident that he will experience God's goodness in his nightmare situation.

REFLECTION

'... everyone deserted him and fled (Mark 14:50): reflect on Jesus' experience of being deserted. Consider too Paul's loneliness in prison while awaiting execution (2 Tim. 4:9–16). Then look at how God strengthened him in that situation (2 Tim. 4:17–18). Like the psalmist, Paul was confident: 'The Lord ... will bring me safely to his heavenly kingdom'.

Confidence in the Lord in the midst of trouble

David calls on God's faithfulness and righteousness (v. 1). He recognises his own sinfulness and his failure to meet God's standard (v. 2). He knows he has no basis for demanding God's help, no basis for negotiation with God. Like all of us, he has no deposit of merit in God's bank on which to draw. Instead, he realises how much he depends on God's mercy rather his own goodness (v. 1).

As he remembers God's goodness in the past (v. 5), David cries out to God like one who is dying of thirst in the desert (v. 6). He longs for some tangible evidence that God still loves him (v. 8) He needs help *now* (v. 7)! He has several specific requests. David prays that when he wakes up the next morning, God will guide him in the decisions he has to make (vv. 8, 10), and that God will rescue him (v. 9), preserve his life and bring him through this time of trouble (v. 11). Finally, he asks God to silence and destroy those who are out to destroy him (v. 12).

Central to the psalm is David's willingness to wait – and to trust. As he waits and prays, he also confirms his commitment to the Lord: 'I am your servant' (v. 12). Though this psalm begins with David's troubles, it ends looking forward to the way ahead with God.

REFLECTION

Like David, when we pray to God, we can be confident that we are not mouthing empty words which float off into the universe. Our confidence in prayer is founded on confidence in the character of God as he has revealed himself to us. He is faithful and righteous (vv. 1, 11), and steadfastly loving (v. 12). All David's prayers in this psalm are bracketed within this knowledge of God. We trust in God and pray to God through Christ: he is God's eternal Son who trusts and obeys his heavenly Father, and we trust and obey the same heavenly Father through him.

A song of deliverance

In this seventh in the series of eight psalms of David (Ps. 138–145), he is still in trouble and in need of rescue. But this psalm is not a cry for help. Rather it's a confident song of praise to the loving Lord and an appreciation of the privilege of knowing and trusting God: 'blessed is the people whose God is the LORD' (v. 15). Many of the verses and themes of this psalm seem to have been copied from other psalms (especially Psalm 18).

David begins with praise and thankfulness to God for giving him so many victories and protecting him (vv. 1–2). He then pauses to reflect with amazement that God should care for human beings, 'mere mortals' (v. 3), whose life passes so quickly like a breath: 'their days are like a fleeting shadow' (v. 4).

Next, in poetic language, he asks God to reach down from on high to rescue him (vv. 5–8). He wants to sing a fresh song to God who has given him victory yet again (vv. 9–10).

He prays again for deliverance and looks forward to the outcomes of God's saving act, a scene of blessing and prosperity which starts with family:

- children will grow and flourish (v. 12);

- food will be enjoyed in abundance (v. 13); and

- a peaceful society will exist: there will be no attacks from enemies causing fear in the streets and 'no going into captivity' (v. 14).

David is thankful for the good gifts of God, but he ends the psalm remembering that he values above all else his relationship with God and the security that brings – a security which lasts (v. 15).

REFLECTION

Notice how intensely personal is David's faith relationship with the Lord: he is 'my Rock ... my loving God and my fortress, my stronghold and my deliverer, my shield, in whom I take refuge' (vv. 1–2, my emphasis). Let's praise and thank God for all his goodness to us.

Unbroken praise

This is one of many praise psalms, but surprisingly the only one specifically given the title 'a psalm of praise'. It is the last from the pen of King David.

It begins with an expressed desire and commitment to praise God every day and forever. This is much more than religious duty. It springs from a deep, God-given longing to give thanks and praise to the King of all the earth.

Why this desire to praise God? In the first half of the psalm (vv. 3–13) David focuses on God's power and goodness. In the second half (vv. 14–21) he celebrates God's faithfulness. The psalm shifts from personal commitment (vv. 1–2) to the bigger picture. David recognises that there is an unbroken chain of praise to God around the world and in every generation (v. 4): 'They speak of the glorious splendour of your majesty' (v. 5); 'They tell of the power of your awesome works' (v. 6); 'They celebrate your abundant goodness' (v. 7); 'They tell of the glory of your kingdom' (v. 11).

As David is caught up in wonder at the greatness of God, he reminds us that the Lord is 'gracious and compassionate, slow to anger and rich in love' (v. 8).

He is good (v. 9). His rule is glorious and everlasting (vv. 11, 13). He is also faithful to his people and to his promises (v. 13). What does that mean in practice? He holds up those who fall (v. 14); he provides for our needs (v. 15); he is righteous in all he does (v. 17); he is near and hears our prayers (v. 18); he fulfils our deepest longings (v. 19); and he watches over us (v. 20). Notice the repeated word 'all'. He 'is trustworthy in *all* his promises and faithful in *all* he does' (v. 13, my italics). He 'is righteous in *all* his ways' (v. 17). He 'upholds *all* who fall and lifts up *all* who are bowed down' (v. 14) – with worry, fear, depression or sickness. He 'is near to *all* who call on him' (v. 18).

REFLECTION

As David ponders what God is like and how he has experienced God's goodness throughout his troubled life, no wonder he ends, as he began, with a deep desire to praise this wonderful God (v. 21).

Who do you trust?

This is the first of a group of five psalms which appropriately close out the book of psalms on a note of praise. All five begin and end with the call: 'Praise the LORD'. Let's note again that 'the LORD' is not a general term for an unknown deity or spiritual power, but the personal name of God, Yahweh, revealed to Moses. The God who created all things (v. 6) and the 'God of Jacob' (v. 5), who delivered Israel from slavery, made a covenant with them and revealed himself to them.

There is no cry for help or desperate prayer in any of this group of psalms, but behind the praise lies life's biggest question: who do you trust when the chips are down? Human leaders may promise much, but they, like all of us, live for a while and then die. Their plans and good intentions die with them at the moment of their death (vv. 3–4). But, by total contrast, the Lord God – the creator of all life, and the maker of heaven and earth – 'remains faithful for ever' (v. 6). Those who trust in him are blessed (v. 5).

This is why the Lord is so worthy of our trust and praise. He is gracious and compassionate: to the oppressed, the prisoners, the hungry, the blind, the 'bowed down', the foreigner, the fatherless and the widow (vv. 7–9). As we read the four gospels in the New Testament, we see the Lord Jesus Christ showing each of these qualities in his dealings with people. His three years of ministry changed the world.

The psalm ends with the encouraging reminder of the truths we have seen recurring many times in the psalms: God, who is just, 'frustrates the ways of the wicked' (v. 9) and he reigns for ever (v. 10).

REFLECTION

Why not take a moment to reflect on God's goodness and mercy to you through Jesus Christ our Saviour, and commit to praising and trusting him as long as you live (v. 2).

Our great and gracious God

A striking feature of this song of praise is how the focus alternates between the greatness of God the Creator and the grace of God. So, for example, verse 3 is about God's grace to the broken-hearted and wounded, but the very next verse is about his unfathomable greatness in making the stars. It's a wonderful reminder that the God who made the whole universe can certainly deal with all our problems on this earth, and we can safely bring them to him in prayer.

Again, verse 6 is about God's grace to the humble, and his rejection of the wicked, but verses 8–9 are about his power over the weather and his goodness in providing food for his creatures. Then comes a very personal insight into the character of God: he doesn't get great enjoyment from the displays of strength and power that typically impress human beings so much (v. 10). Rather he does take great delight 'in those who fear him, who put their hope in his unfailing love' (v. 11). God desires a relationship with us above all else.

This psalm also focuses on the local community of Jerusalem (vv. 2, 12), the place where God set his name (1 Kgs. 8:16–19), and on the special privilege of the people of Israel to whom he revealed his law (v. 19) and to whom he sent the Messiah.

God is the Lord of the Covenant as well as the Lord of Creation. Just as God sends the snow, the hail and rain, so he sends out his word to all the earth. Our God has spoken to us in creation, in the Scriptures and in the person of Jesus. He wants us to hear his voice, if only we are willing to listen (vv. 15–19).

REFLECTION

You don't have to be musical to echo the opening words of this psalm. All who have come to know God through responding to his invitation to come and trust him will know 'How good it is to sing praises to our God' (v. 1).

 **DAY 54**

Songs of praise

Before I became a Christian, I found it very difficult to sing songs of praise to God. If I attended a church for a wedding or funeral, I would stand silent, unable or not wanting to join in the singing. When God awakens our spirits with his Spirit, one of the first changes that he makes is to give us a desire to praise him. It's a longing that comes from deep within the heart.

The book of psalms ends with these three great songs of praise. Like all the best Christian songs, they engage both our minds and our hearts. They express truth about God and his great salvation, and stir up our emotions to respond to his goodness to us.

In **Psalm 148** there is a progression downwards from the heavens to the creation (vv. 1–6). Then there is a corresponding upward movement of thought from the sea to the storms, the mountains, the wildlife, humankind, and their leaders and rulers (vv. 7–12). The message is the same throughout: let all God's creation praise the Lord for 'his name alone is exalted' (v. 13), as Creator of all and Redeemer of his people (v. 14).

While Psalm 148 urges the whole creation to praise God, **Psalm 149** is a call to 'his faithful people' (v. 1).

Worship in the psalms is certainly not boring: the psalmist encourages joyful dancing and music in celebration of what God has done (vv. 2–3). There is much to celebrate: 'For the LORD takes delight in his people; he crowns the humble with victory. Let his faithful people rejoice in this honour' (vv. 4–5).

Finally, **Psalm 150** calls us – and 'everything that has breath' (v. 6), accompanied by every imaginable musical instrument (vv. 3–5) – to praise God. We are to praise him in his sanctuary and in the heavens (v. 1), and to praise him for 'his acts of power' and 'his surpassing greatness' (v. 2).

REFLECTION

'Praise the LORD'! Those are the last words in this wonderful book of psalms. Take a few moments to praise God now for who he is and for all he has done for us in Jesus Christ. Pray that many people from every nation would come to praise God in Christ.

REFERENCES

1 See J. B. Philips' translation: The New Testament in Modern English, copyright © 1960, 1972 J. B. Phillips. Administered by The Archbishops' Council of the Church of England. Used by Permission.

2 From James Montgomery's hymn 'Forever with the Lord!' (1835).

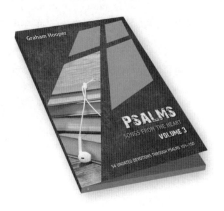

10Publishing is the publishing house of **10ofThose**. It is committed to producing quality Christian resources that are biblical and accessible.

www.10ofthose.com is our online retail arm selling thousands of quality books at discounted prices.

For information contact: **sales@10ofthose.com** or check out our website: **www.10ofthose.com**